3 Day Guide to Venice

A 72-hour definitive guide on what to see, eat and enjoy in Venice, Italy

3 DAY CITY GUIDES

D1343095

Image use under CC-BY License via Flickrr

Cover Photo Credits:

Frank Kovalchek Close up of bright red mask

Oliver Clarke Murano

O Palsson Laundry day in Venice

gnuckx Gondolas at Hotel Ca' Sagredo

ISBN: 1505432979
ISBN-13: 978-1505432978

"Our happiest moments as tourists always seem to come when we stumble upon one thing while in pursuit of something else." — Lawrence Block

CONTENTS

1 INTRODUCTION TO VENICE

Venice Canal, Italy. Photo by <u>Artur Staszewski</u>

The story of Venice is very unique, in every sense of the word. The only one of its kind in the world, you will be amazed by the magnificent edifices dotting the banks of its canals. Each structure within the city is rich in history, marking an extravagant lifestyle enjoyed by the Venetians in the height of their wealth. Observe Venice's old glory days with all its pomp and splendor as Venetians rose from work as simple fishermen doing trade along the banks of the Grand Canal, to become wealthy businessmen. Their hard work earned them a niche in world-class trading and commerce due to the city's strategic maritime location. They built their palaces, castles and houses in this floating Italian city until Venice fell from her grand stature in the 18th century.

Today, only traces of the fame and grandeur of a bygone era can be seen in the city's landmarks. Almost every place in Venice; the palazzos, the piazzas, its alleys and canals, speaks of what life was like when the Venetians had it all. As you explore the city and its inner alleys, you will traverse a route where the mighty and gracious Venetian nobilities once resided. Every nook and cranny serving as a silent witness to what was once; a majestic era.

It is indeed true that there's more to Venice than meets the eye. Beyond the romantic escapades that Venice has been known for, this place has undoubtedly, more stories to tell.

Abundant art and architectural treasures stand proudly amidst a very unique setting. This magical floating city is surrounded by water from all sides and within as it sits on an archipelago of small islands; 118 islets grouped together in this northern side of Italy. The main thoroughfares are not streets, but canals. Narrow passageways are used by pedestrians for walking. There are 177 canals in the city which provide transportation routes. These canals are spanned by more than 400 bridges, most of which are arched to allow boats to pass beneath. Traditional boats traverse these canals which are called "gondolas". But in the recent years, power boats are now a faster way of conveyance. The entire city, including its lagoon, are listed as a

World Heritage Site.

Venice is the hometown of the explorer Marco Polo and the great musical composer, Antonio Vivaldi. It is also known as the city of Casanova, the famous Italian adventurer and writer during the 18th century, known for his complicated and elaborate love affairs with women. In Shakespeare's Romeo and Juliet, Venice is also included as the site where Othello married a Venetian named Desmoneda.

When people think of Venice, images of flirtatious rendezvous, comes to mind. But as you set foot here, you will immediately be intrigued by how this place came to be, making you hungry to know more. The depth of facts surrounding its emergence, its rise and fall from power, and the transition to becoming one of the world's sought-after tourist destinations will leave you completely enthralled.

History

There are no historical records that deal directly with the founding of Venice, but it is believed that its history dates back to 421 AD when a Byzantine Duke moved his patriarchal seat to what is now known as the Rialto. At first, the inhabitants who were mainly farmers fleeing the bandits, built their houses on the unstable marshes of the lagoon, and lived by fishing and salt trade. Due to the city's geographical location, Venetians were predestined to be sailors. At that time, Venice was granted the city trading rights along the Adriatic coast.

In 828, the claimed relics of St. Mark the

Evangelist, the city's known patron saint, were acquired and placed in the new basilica. From the 9th to the 12th century, Venice developed into a city state and maintained its strategic position in naval and commercial power. The city became a flourishing trade center between Western Europe and the rest of the world. It was said that affluence and fortune marks the early Venetians' way of life.

Most of the people here were rich and powerful. Venice became an imperial power following the Fourth Crusade (Crusades were military campaigns sanctioned by the Latin Roman Catholic Church aimed to wage defensive war against Islamic conquest as part of a long-running conflict at the frontiers of Europe). Situated on the Adriatic Sea, Venice always traded extensively with the Byzantine Empire and the Muslim world.

The Republic of Venice was a major maritime power during the Middle Ages and Renaissance, and a staging area for the Crusades and the Battle of Lepanto, as well as a very important center of commerce (especially silk, grain, and spice) and art in the 13th century up to the end of the 17th century. This made Venice a wealthy city throughout most of its history.

Napoleon Bonaparte, the great French commander conquered Venice in 1797. The French conqueror brought to an end the most fascinating century of its history. During the 18th century, Venice became perhaps the most elegant and refined city in Europe, greatly influencing art, architecture and literature. Napoleon was seen as something of a liberator by the city's Jewish population by his act of removing the gates of the Ghetto and ending the restrictions of when and where Jews could live and travel in the city.

In 1848–1849, a revolt briefly reestablished the Venetian Republic under Daniele Manin. In 1866, following the Third Italian War of Independence, Venice, along with the rest of the Veneto, became part of the newly created Kingdom of Italy.

During the Second World War, the historic city was largely free from attack, the only aggressive effort of note being Operation Bowler, a successful Royal Air Force precision strike on the German naval operations there in March 1945. The targets were destroyed with virtually no architectural damage done to the city itself.

On 29 April 1945, New Zealand troops reached Venice and relieved the city and the mainland, which were already in partisan hands. Fortunately, the city was spared extreme structural damage during the war and it was able to retain its impressive structures. On November 4, 1966, disaster struck. Record floods poured into 16,000 Venetian homes, stranding residents in the wreckage of 1400 years of civilization. Once again, Venice's cosmopolitan nature saved it as assistance from all over the world poured in to redress the ravages of the flood. Today, with 60,000 official residents, easily outnumbered by day-trippers,

Venetians may seem scarce in their own city. The city remains relevant and realistic, continuing to produce new music, art and crafts even as it seeks sustainable solutions to rising water levels. The city remains anchored not just by the ancient pylons, but by the undaunted spirit of its people.

Foundations

Many often wonder how the structures in Venice were built – in water, that is. This has been one of the architectural wonders of all time. These structures are not just small houses, but grand palaces or palazzos, castles and basilicas. The location for the city of Venice was chosen out of necessity. It was occupied by a group of merchants trying to escape barbarian attacks in the northern region of the country. They found an archipelago formed out of 120 submerged islands. They built their first houses on the marshes, but were forced to find a better solution.

The buildings of Venice are constructed on closely-spaced wooden piles (larch pylons). Most of these piles are still intact after centuries of submersion. The foundations rest on the piles. Over time, the pylons petrified. Most of these piles were made from trunks of alder trees, a wood noted for its water resistance. Submerged by water, in oxygen-poor conditions, this type of wood does not decay as rapidly as on the surface.   Slabs of Istrian stone, similar to marble, but much stronger, were placed over them. The piles penetrate a softer layer of sand and mud until they reach a much harder layer of compressed clay. These were the foundations of the future buildings of the city.

The Landmarks

Venetians rely on tourism as a source of income. The floating city takes pride in its museums, monuments, and churches, which are considered a valuable part of the artistic global treasury. Throughout history, the city's local artists have been unmatched in their mastery of creating the perfect mirrors, stained glass, and upholstery. They decorated the city and helped spread its fame to the distant corners of the world. Ca' Dario Palace is the strangest landmark in the city as it is believed to be cursed. It has become famous due to the series of unexplainable deaths of its owners, which started when it was built back in 1847.

Venice is a fascinating city that attracts millions of visitors from all over the world, drawn here by its narrow streets, romantic gondola rides, unique landmarks, and legends. Ever since it was built over the waters of the Adriatic, it was predestined to be a curiosity, an impressive and mysterious location that has no other rival in the world. Navigating the labyrinthine streets and canals of Venice can be a challenge, even with a map. But, the most wonderful aspect of this city is that it allows you to throw yourself into an unforgettable adventure, getting lost and finding your way through this magical floating city.

Climate

Venice has a Mediterranean climate which means that they have warm to hot, dry summers and mild to cool, wet winters although Venice is mostly wet throughout the year. Due its location on the Adriatic coast, Venice often experiences thunderstorms and rain showers which tend to cause flooding. Known as the "acqua alta", which is a Venetian term for high water, it usually occurs during November and December and is the result of tidal activity. Venice created "Mose" which is a special engineering project aimed to fight "acqua alta". The project utilizes a system of barriers that are placed to keep the water from flooding the city.

Spring

Spring takes place between the months of March until the end of May. Average daytime temperatures in spring range from around 12°C (53°F) at the start of the season and reaches up to 21°C (70°F) as the summer approaches. During the night, the average temperature drops to 5°C (41°F).

Summer

Venice endures hot weather during the summer months of June, peaking in July and August. Temperatures usually range between 86°F to 91°F (30°C to 33°C). During this season, the days are long and the nights are warm. However, weather in

Venice is unpredictable and that means that even during the hot summer months, rain can still fall. July and August are also the busiest time of the year as these are the peak months for tourists.

Autumn

This is a wonderful time to go to Venice. The months of September, October and November are the most pleasant months in terms of weather. The autumn weather is mild with occasional winds. Tourist crowds are thinning, prices and temperatures are dropping and the food is fantastic. October generally brings crisp, cold air in the mornings and in the evenings, but it's still sunny during the day. November however, is the month with the heaviest rainfall before the snow starts to fall in December.

Winter

Winter season is from December to February. Temperatures drop to between 32°F and 37°F (0°C to 3°C). December is the coldest month while January gets only 5°C of average high. In fact, winter weather remains chilly for the visitors with the average low of -09°C in January. Tourist should bring warm coat, a pair of thick gloves and so on to be protected from cold winter.

Best Time to Visit

Each season in Venice has its magic, but the city is at its best during late spring , April to May, and early summer, in June. These are the months when there are fewer crowds. The town exudes tranquility and silence, giving you the serenity of enjoying this piece of heaven, all on your own. You may also opt to go and visit Venice in winter. It may be chilly, but the charms of the city are untouched by the weather.

Whatever season you may choose to pick for a Venice holiday, it is best to pack waterproof shoes or boots to avoid a soaking. Spring, summer and autumn are all considered peak tourist season in Venice, with April to October, being the busiest time in the city. However, it is a popular destination all year round and can get uncomfortably crowded. Christmas, Easter, Carnival (in February) and the Venice International Film Festival (in August) are also busy periods.

Language

Veneto is the native language of the Venetians. This is an Italian dialect, but differs in Italian in grammar, phonetics, and vocabulary. This language is classified as a Western Romance language, which Italian is a not a part of. Generally, the people of Venice can speak English too.

Getting In

All major airlines fly into Marco Polo Airport, located 7 kilometers north of the city. The main reseller of public transport tickets, Hello Venezia, which also issues passes (pre-ordered online) can easily be found within the vicinity of the airport. Major transportation hosts are there upon your exit from the baggage claim area. Travel to the city and other destinations on the mainland is available immediately outside the arrival halls, on the ground level.

There are several ways to reach Venice from the airport.

Private Water Taxi

If you have heavy luggages, you may opt to hire a private water taxi which can take you directly to your hotel and can be booked upon your arrival. The hire charge includes up to 4 passengers and all their luggages. All water taxis are metered and you should not pay more than €80 - 120, depending on how far you are travelling. Note you should never be quoted a price per passenger. For advance booking, you may go to :

www.motoscafivenezia.it .

Land Route to Venice

Taxis

There are taxis available right outside the Marco Polo airport. You just need to ask them to bring you to Venice.

Buses

There are two reasonable bus options. ACTV local bus scheduled service No. 5 and ATVO direct coaches. Both will take you to Piazzale Roma in 20-25 minutes, depending on the traffic conditions. Piazzale Roma is the end of the road in historic Venice. You will then need to utilize ACTV water buses to take you around Venice.

Train

It's possible to travel from London to Venice by train in one day, by Eurostar, TGV and Italian domestic train in a little less than 15 hours. By taking the first Eurostar of the day you can be in Paris by mid-morning, where high-speed TGVs depart 3 times per day towards Milan. However, unless you stop-off in Paris overnight, just one of the TGVs is a practical choice. Take a Eurostar Italia train from Milan Centrale to Venice Santa Lucia, which has a journey time of just 2 hours 35 mins between stations.

In addition to the high-speed train, there are regional Milan to Venice trains that make the journey in 3 hours 30 mins, but if you can book in advance the Eurostar Italia service is both cheap and efficient. Booking for the Eurostar Italia opens 3 months in advance, while the booking horizon on Italian regional trains is 90 days.

For more information, you may visit: http://www.seat61.com/Europe-train-travel.htm#.VBOnN_mSzKM

Getting Around

The best way to explore Venice is on foot. You will enjoy walking around its narrow, winding alleys (called "Calli" or "Calle") which across many little squares, dotted with small shops, as well as souvenir stores selling a wide variety of goods from purses to belts, glasses and more.

As Venice is primarily a city in waters (actually, a series of small islands sitting on a lagoon), you need to hop on/off their water transportation to get from one place to another. Venice has a very efficient public transportation system run by ACTV. These are various-sized "vaporetto" boats (water buses). These boats run on a schedule and there are connecting lines should you wish to travel to outlying islands such as Lido, Giudecca, Murano, BUrano, Torcello and others. They also have trips during nightime.

For details such as rates and schedules, visit: http://www.actv.it/en/movinginvenice/prices

The Venetian Boats

The Venetian boats, or the gondolas, are the traditional means of transportation in this city. Each of these elegant boats are handcrafted by traditional Venetian craftsmen, sculpted from eight different types of wood. Although they might look symmetrical, all gondolas hide a little imperfection. Their left side is taller than the right by exactly 9.4 inches. The gondolas are inspired by the city itself, and its components represent the main sections in Venice, like the six neighborhoods, Giudecca Island, and the Rialto Bridge. There are only 400 licensed gondoliers in Venice.

Traghetto or Traghetti

These are "ferry" boats plying on the Grand Canal. It crosses this waterway at seven points between the railroad station and St. Mark's Basin. These are the primary mode of transportation which takes the locals to their destinations across the islands. There are no bow decoration, brocaded chairs, and other luxury trimmings. The fare is more reasonable than gondolas.

The routes are clearly marked on any good street map of Venice (straight lines across the Grand Canal), and you'll see yellow lines pointing toward the traghetto landings. These are small wooden pier along the edge of the Grand Canal. Boats shuttle back and forth almost continuously, so you shouldn't have to wait long.

Upon boarding, find a place to sit or stand. Face backward, because the boat will turn as it leaves the dock (Venetians traditionally stand during the crossing). Hand your fare to the oarsman as you board or leave the boat..

2 VENICE DAY 1

For most trips in any city, province or town for that matter, the first day is the most exciting. It is simply because the eagerness of discovery is very high. Being new to the place, there's simply a lot to see, and explore. The suggested first day itinerary below will take you to the impressive museums showcasing medieval, Renaissance as well as contemporary art pieces, the famous Piazza San Marco, and the former place of residence of the head of Venice, the Doge. To cap a hectic day, you can spend a night watching a memorable operatic performance.

But before you head off to the first destination, you may opt to have breakfast in one of the oldest bakeries in Venice. Pasticceria Rosa Salva has a large selection of typical Venetian cakes, cookies, brioches, rolls, sandwiches, tramezzeni (a typical Venetian triangle soft bread sandwich), fritters, meringues, millefeuilles and much more. Perfect to pair with a shot of espresso and voila, you're ready to go.

Pasticceria Rosa Salva
Campo SS Giovanni e Paolo
Tel: +39 (0)41 5227949

Gallerie dell'Accademia

A ceiling of a room in the Gallerie dell'accademia.
Photo by Sailko

Duration: 3 hours

One of the world's great museums, Gallerie dell'Accademia is something that you should not miss on your trip to Venice. Right at the very entrance of the Accademia, you will be enthralled by the huge wooden arch of the Ponte dell Accademia. From the top of the bridge, you get to see an exhilarating view of the Grand Canal, gazing down at the church of Sta. Maria della Salute, the Bacino di San Marco and the Punta della Dogana. The grand collection of timeless masterpieces (European and Venetian paintings) are all housed here.

See breathtaking works of arts by Bellini, Carpaccio
and a lot more. Main features are religious and
Rennaisance art. The 24 rooms in this structure
gathers visual drama, intrigue, passion, and
romance depicted in each stroke, in every color, in
every creation.

Room 1 has works by the earliest recorded Venetian
painters, including Paol Veneziano and Lorenzo
Veneziano (the soubriquet indicates 'school of
Venice' rather than any blood ties between the two).

Moving to Room 2, you will encounter works from
late 15th and early 16th centuries, including pieces
by Giovanni Bellini, Cima da Conegliano, and
Carpaccio's Crucifixion and Glorification of the Ten
Thousand Martyrs of Mount Ararat.

Room 3, 4 and 5 have a selection of works from the
early Renaissance in Venice; Giogione's Tempest;
series of Madonnas by Giovanni Bellini and
Mantegna's St George.

Room 6 includes The Creation of the Animals by
Tintoretto (Jacopo Robusti) and John the Baptist
by Titian (Tiziano Vecellio), while Room 7 includes
Young Man in His Study by Lorenzo Lotto. Rooms
8 and 9 focus on the 16th century, while Room 10
has Paolo Veronese's Christ in the House of Levi.
Works by Tintoretto, including The Thief of the

Body of St Mark, St Marks Saves a Saracen and St Mark Rescues a Slave.

Room 11 includes works by Giambattista Tiepolo include The Translation of the Holy House of Loreto and Tintoretto's Madonna dei Tesorieri. You will pass through more works from the 15th, 16th and 17th centuries, with high points being Alvise Vivarini's Santa Chiara, Giovanni Bellini's series of triptychs and brother Gentile Bellini's Blessed Lorenzo Giustinian.

Enter Room 20 and you'll find the marvellous Cure of a Lunatic and the Story of St Ursula (a complete cycle of works) by Carpaccio. Gentile Bellini is represented by Recovery of the Relic from the Canale di San Lorenzo and then Procession of the relic in the Piazza.

Room 24 houses Titian's Presentation of the Virgin, and a triptych by Antonio Vivarini and Giovanni d'Alemagna.

Address: Campo della Carita, Dorsoduro n 1050, 30130 Venice
Telephone: +39 041 5200345
Opening Hours: Monday – 8:00AM to 2:00PM; Tuesday to Sunday – 8:15AM to 7:15 PM
Rates: Ticket prices are €15 (+ €1.5 reservation fee) but there is a host of conditions allowing reduced or free entrance into the galleries, and several days with discounted entrance. During special temporary exhibitions the price of admission is

subject to change. For more detailed information, the Gallerie dell'Accademia website has frequent updates. For more information, you may visit: http://www.gallerieaccademia.org/?lang=en

Peggy Guggenheim Collection

Duration: 2-3 hours

A wealthy American heiress, Peggy Guggenheim was an art curator. When she lost her father in the Titanic in 1912, she befriended Dadaists, dodged Nazis and changed art history at her palatial home on the grand canal. She built this museum in Venice which features her exquisite and remarkable art collection, all of which were chosen based on her own convictions rather than prestige or style. This include some 200 breakthrough masterpieces of modern/contemporary artists, including Peggy's ex-husband Max Ernst and Jackson Pollock.

Acclaimed to be one of the most important museums in Italy, it is also one of the most visited spots in city. Most of the artworks embraces Cubism, Surrealism and Abstract Expressionism. Peggy lived in Venice until her death in 1979. Her ashes are interred in the garden of her home, next to her beloved dogs.

Address: Street Palazzo Venier dei Leoni 704
Telephone: +390 41 240 54 11
Opening Hours: 10am-6pm Wed-Mon

Tickets
Adults: € 10
Senior visitors over 65 yrs.: € 8
Students under 26 yrs.: € 5 (with current student
ID) Children under 10 yrs.: free

For more information, you may visit:
http://www.guggenheim-
venice.it/inglese/museum/info_biglietteria.html

Saint Mark's Basilica (Basilica di San Marco)

Inside the Basilica. Photo by HarshLight

Duration: 1-2 hours

This magnificent structure blends architectural masterpieces of the east and the west. With its Italian-Byzantine architecture, it lies on the eastern side of Piazza San Marco, adjacent to the Doge's Palace. Originally, it was the chapel of the Doge, but it became the city's only cathedral in 1807, serving as the seat of the Patriarch of Venice. Here is where St. Mark's relics lies. In the first half of the 13th century, the new façade was constructed and most of the mosaics were completed. The domes were covered with a set of higher domes of lead-covered wood to match that of the Gothic architecture of the Doge's Palace.

The exterior design features marble columns, bronze-fashioned doors, and other pieces from the 18th and 19th century. The stone sculpture is at the lower level, where a forest of columns and patterned marble slabs are the main emphases. It includes narrow bands of Romanesque work on the portals, richly carved borders of foliage mixed with figures to the ogee arches and other elements, and large shallow relief saints between the arches. Along the roofline, by contrast, there is a line of statues, many in their own small pavilions, culminating to Saint Mark flanked by six angels in the centre, above a large gilded winged lion (his symbol, and that of Venice).

The interior is based on a Greek cross, with each arm divided into three naves with a dome of its own. It has five domes in all. The marble floor has geometric patterns and animal designs. The upper level of the interiors are completely covered with bright mosaics with traditional gold glass tesserae as a background, creating an overall shimmering effect.

The canopy over the high altar is made of gold decorated with precious gems, sitting on columns decorated with 11th century reliefs. Byzantine goldsmiths were hired during the 10th century to complete this work.

You may also take note of the statue of the Four Tetrarchs, taken from Constantinople in 1204. They say that this represents the inter-dependence of the four Roman rulers.

The treasury is situated at the right of the main altar. It contains many items taken from Constantinople as well as other relics the church has gathered over the years. The collection include the famous Horses of Saint Mark which are four life-sized bronze sculptures dating back to Greco-Roman times.

Opulent designs, gold round mosaics, this basilica, together with all the structures in the Piazza San Marco stands as the symbol of Venetian wealth and power.

St. Mark's Square (Piazza San Marco)

Duration: 1-2 hours

Venice's heart lies in this place and it is considered to be one of the most beautiful squares in the world. The L-shaped piazza is filled with centuries of history and has even been referred to as the drawing board of Europe. The basilica is at one end and the Campanile bell tower is located in the middle. The elegantly-adorned Doge's Palace sits close by, adjacent to the basilica. This square undoubtedly showcases memories of the Venetian aristocracy.

A prominent structure in the square are the two tall columns along the waterfront which represent Venice's two patron saints. The column of San Marco is topped with a winged lion while the column of San Teodoro holds up a statue of Saint Theodore.

At this point, you may feel a bit tired already and ready to take a break. No need to worry, you're in the best place to sit down and relax. Piazza San Marco has spots when you can have a brief respite. You can even take sometime off to grab a coffee, munch on a few snacks, feed the pigeons and enjoy the pleasant view.

St Mark's Square. Photo by Elliott Brown

Doge's Palace

Duration: 1 hour

Pallazo Ducale, or Doge's Palace was the seat of power of Venice for centuries. The elected ruler of Venice, the Doge, lived here. Law courts, civil administration, bureaucracy and the jail (until it was relocated across the Bridge of Sighs), are all located inside this edifice.

It stands proudly parallel to the waterfront, with the grand entrance built by Giovanni and Bartolomeo Bon in 1438, as commissioned by the Doge, Francesco Foscari.

The entrance to this majestic palace is through a door next to the Lagoon where you will enter into an enormous courtyard. This palace has a mix of architectural styles and influence, from Renaissance classicism to Gothic. The decor is elaborate and the 36 capitals of the building have carvings of beasts, flowers and representations of the months of the year. Huge walls of white limestone and pink marble are combined with porticos (a structure consisting of a roof supported by columns at regular intervals), finely wrought loggias, (a gallery or room with one or more open sides, especially one that forms part of a house and has one side open to the garden), crenellated roofs (for purposes of defense where one can shoot guns and cannons against attacking enemies) and a series of balconies (for addressing the people).

Doge's Palace. Photo by ncrob1

The palace's most impressive room, the Sala del

Maggior Consiglio (the Hall of the Great Council) is a must-see. It has paintings of the first 76 doges except for one – Marino Faliero, the 55th doge of Vienna who attempted to stage a coup to declare himself a prince. He underwent trial, pleaded guilty, and was given a punishment of death, mutilation and condemnation. His place on the wall of paintings is empty, and is covered by a black veil.

Location: Piazza de San Marco
Hours: Daily 8:30 – 7:00 (closes 5:30 in winter)
Telephone No. : Tel. (0039) 041-2715-911
Admission: €16 (as of 2012) for Saint Mark's Square Museums Pass, includes 3 other museums. Reduced price for over age 65, be sure to ask at ticket window. Doge's Palace is also included in the 11-museum pass, good for a longer period.

Musica a Palazzo

Duration: 1-2 hours

After a tiring day the city's art and cultural heritage sites, it's time to unwind and relax. Witness world-class performances in the 15th century Palazzo Barbarigo-Minotto on Fondamebda Duodo o Barbarigo in San Marco sestiere.

How to get there? All you need to do is walk from San Marco towards Accademia. You will see a sign directing you to turn left. It will then lead you towards two bridges, one will bring you to

Accademia, while the left one will bring you to the palace. The most beautiful voices accompanied by several instruments will serenade you amidst a splendid backdrop. Here 19th-century operas such as Verdi's La Traviata and Rossini's The Barber of Seville are performed, among others. These performances are done without a stage, with the audience becoming part of the scene. This is will be an extraordinary, unique and intimate experience that will let you feel every part of the story from within.

Address : Street Palazzo Barbarigo-Minotto, Fondamenta Barbarigo o Duodo 2504
Telephone: +390 340 971 72 72
Price: Tickets incl beverage €60

3 VENICE DAY 2

The second day spent in Venice will take you to more interesting places, reveal the story behind them and allow you to appreciate the experience learned from such discoveries. Your itinerary will include seeing the famous Rialto Bridge, a unique museum, a less-travelled path to the district of Dorsoduro and a visit to a theatre which had survived through several fires.

Before proceeding to the said places, why not begin this interesting day with breakfast in Cafe Florian, located in Piazza San Marco. It has been a favorite of locals and tourists alike for decades and is the oldest cafe in Italy.

Cafe Florian is best known for late breakfast or early lunch (brunch). They offer a full menu of delectable dishes, delicious pastries and breads that pair well with their selection of coffee and tea.

Rialto Bridge (Ponte di Rialto)

The Rialto Bridge. Photo by <u>Steve Parker</u>

Duration: 1 hour

The most famous bridge that crosses the Grand Canal in Venice, Ponte di Rialto, a stone arch, was constructed under the supervision of Antonio da Ponte, between 1588 and 1591. For almost three hundred years, it was the only way to cross the Grand Canal on foot. The original structure was made of wood and did not last long. Thus, the bridge was reconstructed using a sturdier material. Today, the stone bridge is formed by two inclined ramps covered by a portico to allow the boats to pass beneath it. Tourists flock to this area to marvel at how this bridge was constructed over water and also, to see the shops lined up on each side of the bridge. It is now acclaimed as the most photographed bridge in Venice.

Dorsoduro

Dorsoduro, Venezia. Photo by Eric Salard

Duration: 2-3 hours

This is the most unpretentious district of Venice which houses picturesque canals and palazzi, and some of the city's great art showcases. This is where you can find numerous attractions such as the Peggy Guggenheim Museum as well as the Accademia, Santa Maria della Salute and more. No tourist traps here, just pure charm. The atmosphere is more of an artistic, youthful and relaxed ambience. The district is perfect to experience the best of Venice by way of a leisurely walk. Dorsoduro is in Central Venice located at the south-western side of the city. Here is where you will see the most attractive stretch of Grand Canal passing under the Accademia Bridge. This is also a student area serving as home to Venice's Ca' Foscari University.

Ca' Rezzonico

Duration: 2-3 hours

One of the lesser known museums in the city, Ca' Rezzonico is packed not only with important art deco pieces carefully preserved for centuries, but also contains memorabilia from the families who occupied this grand palace. The museum is dedicated to exploring and explaining 18th century Venice. It has a complicated and intriguing history, having been passed from one family to another , from one generation to the next. All of them having shared one thing in common: they belong to the most affluent and powerful families in Venice who at one point or another ran out of funds to continue preserving what they had.

Located at the junction of the Grand Canal and the Rio di San Barnaba, the palace has a symmetrical marble facade of plastered, rounded arches. The rusticated ground floor facade has a central recessed, three-bay portico with pediment, flanked by bay windows. On the piano nobile floor, it has seven bays or arched windows, divided by pilasters. The next piano nobile floor has a shallow mezzanine floor of oval windows. Balconies project, slightly accentuating the baroque nature of the facade. Truly, this palace is a great architectural feat.

Address: Dorsoduro, 3136, 30213 Venice
Telephone: +39 041 241 0100
Open: 1/11 - 31/03; 10.00 - 17.00 h.
1/04 - 31/10; 10.00 - 18.00 h
Closed on Tuesdays and on 25th December, 1st
January, 1st May.

Full price 7,00 euro
Reduced 5,00 euro, children aged 6 to 14, students
aged 15 to 25, citizens over 65.

Teatro La Fenice

Duration: 2-3 hours

This is the Theatre of the Phoenix. One of the best-known opera houses in Europe, it has been the site of many premieres. Why was it named after the Phoenix? The original theatre burned down to the ground, six years after it was built in 1790. It was rebuilt and was renamed after the mythical bird which rose from the ashes. The first opera performed here after its reconstruction was Giovani Paisiello's I Giochi di Agrigento. At that time, this theatre attracted a large number of audience from all levels of society.

In 1836, the theatre burned down again and was rebuilt by the architects and brothers Tommaso and Giambasta Meduna. Tragedy struck again in 1996, the third time that this theatre suffered another fire. The third one was due to arson. In 2003, reconstruction started once more and was done in less than 2 years. It was redesigned based on its 19th century style. In December 2003, the inaugural concert included works by Beethoven, Stravinsky and Wagner.

Teatro La Fenice. Photo by Miguel Mendez

Address: Campo San Fantin, 1965, 30124 Venezia, Italy
Telephone: +39 041 786511

For schedule of events and ticket prices, you may visit:http://www.teatrolafenice.it/site/index.php?pag=87&lingua=ENG

4 VENICE DAY 3

The third day of your trip, it will be spent exploring the nearby islands nestled on the lagoon of the city. Each one boasts of its own character and is well-regarded for their arts and crafts. Water taxis can zip you quickly to any of these islands. Ferry boats can also bring you there in a more relaxed and less expensive way.

Torcello

Santa Fosca, Torcello. Photo by François Philipp

Duration: 1-2hours

Musky Torcello is one of the most popular islands to visit in the Venice lagoon. This is the place where Venice was born. Just an half-hour boat ride from the main island, this is the place where the first Venetians settled in the 5th century. Here is where you can find the oldest church in Venice, the Cathedral of Maria Dell' Assunta which was built in 639. Today, you can still see the remnants of its facade. The interiors are still intact with its intricate mosaics which demonstrates the importance of this church to the first Venetians. From the boat stop, the main path leads to the cathedral. It is open daily from 10:00 to 17:30. Admission is 5 euro. The Church of Sta. Fosca (stands next to the Cathedral) is another interesting sight. The Torcello Museum is housed in a 14th century mansion that was once the seat of Venetian government and now houses medieval artifacts, mostly from the island, and archeological finds from the paleolithic age to Roman period.

Should you opt to take your early lunch in this island, you can choose from these restaurants:

Osteria al Ponte del Diavolo (closed Mondays) serves lunches based on fresh, seasonal ingredients and has outdoor seating in a garden.

Ristorante Villa '600 (closed Wednesdays) is housed in a building dating from the 1600's and has an outdoor dining area in a beautiful setting.

Ristorante al Trono di Attila (closed Mondays except in summer) also serves lunch.

Murano

Murano. Photo by <u>Oliver Clarke</u>

Duration: 1-2 hours

Venice is very famous for its glass. In this island along the Venetian lagoon, glass artisans continue to blow glass baubles, considered to be an elite pursuit dominated by local craftsmen. Murano was a prosperous trading center back in the 10th century. In 1291, Venetian Republic ordered the glassmakers to move their foundries to Murano to prevent fire dangers in Venice. It was also said that this was aimed to protect the secret of glassmaking which was a very flourishing and lucrative industry.

Their virtual monopoly of this trade lasted for centuries.

Today, you can see their elaborate shops in this island where you will find sophisticatedly designed products. You can also witness the traditional, elaborate mastery of this craft showcased before your very eyes.

Isola di Burano

Burano. Photo by <u>*netpalantir*</u>

Duration: 1-2 hours

The island of Burano is the place of brightly-colored

houses lining up the canals. Their window boxes are adorned with flowers while boats are docked lazily on the side. This very picturesque island is the home of artisan lace makers. The island is literally dotted with shops selling a product of a tradition which dates back 500 years ago. These laces were painstakingly produced by the ladies of Burano using only needles and threads. They meticulously follow time honored patterns from a tradition that has been passed on from one generation to the next.

Apart from the lace-making attraction, Burano also has a 15th century leaning bell tower in San Martino Church. There is also a Lace Museum that is worth seeing as well. But, the best part of this island can best be seen when the sun begins to set. It is at its most charming at dusk, when you can feel the peacefulness and beauty of this place.

For good views of Burano, get off at the small island of Mazzorbo, the stop just before Burano. Walk across the island from to the pathway where you'll see Burano and then cross at the foot bridge connecting the two islands. On Mazzorbo you can visit the 14th century church of Santa Caterina and there are also a couple of restaurants.

Museo del Merletto

Duration: 1-2 hours

Before you leave the island of Burano, it is recommended to stop by and visit the Lace Museum (Museo del Merletto). This museum tells the story of the craft that have stayed on for centuries. From the triple-petalled corollas of Madonna's mantle in Torcello's 12th-century mosaics, to Queen Margherita's spider web-fine 20th-century mittens. The exhibit showcases not just arts and crafts but a legacy of an age-old tradition depicting the creative expression of female sensitivity, love for fine refinements and an eye for detail.

Telephone: +390 41 4273 0892
 Opening hours: 10am-6pm Tue-Sun Apr-Oct, to 4.30pm Nov-Mar
 Prices: adult/reduced €5/3.50

Grand Canal

Duration: 1-2 hours

Take time to cruise along the Grand Canal, the main traffic corridor of Venice. It has an S-shaped form and dissects the city into two. It travels from Saint Mark Basin on one end to a lagoon near the Santa Lucia rail station on the other. This ancient waterway measures 3,800 meters and ranges from 30 to 90 meters wide. In most places, the canal is approximately 5 meters deep. The Grand Canal played a very important role in Venice history as it has been a silent witness of how trade and commerce flourish during its golden years. Along this waterway, water vessels carrying prized commodities travelled back and forth as merchants conducted business deals from their mansions built strategically along the banks of this canal. Today, lined with beautiful castles, palazzi, and mansions which are mostly converted into museums, it provides a one-of-a-kind scenery that you can only see in Venice. Catch a vaporetto and take in the sights.

The Grand Canal at Sunset. Photo by John Fowler

5 BEST PLACES (EAT, WINE & DINE)

Venice is proud of its fresh marine catch and this is very evident in its culinary masterpieces. Most restaurants offer the best seafood prepared in a variety of dishes.

Trattoria Alla Madonna, Venice. Photo by Italy Chronicles Photos

Fiaschetteria Toscana

It is worth a visit for its courteous service, fine but

conventional, no surprises cooking and ample cellar. Gastronomic highlights include light tagliolini neri al ragu di astice (thin black noodles served with a delicate lobster sauce). Feast on these sumptuous gastronomic delights amidst an elegant setting.

Cannaregio, 5719
Venezia, Italy
+39 041 528 5281

Antiche Carampane

Venice is a seafood island where Italian chefs whip up the best culinary masterpieces using the freshest bounty from the sea. One restaurant that serves the best seafood cuisine is located right at the heart of Venice, only steps away from the Rialto Bridge, this famous seafood restaurant has been a favorite establishment of politicians and celebrities. Top choices are Tagliatelle with scallops and pesto, spaghetti with clams, grilled seafoods, lemon tarts for dessert.

Sestiere San Polo, 1911
Venezia, Italy
+39 041 524 0165

Trattoria alla Madonna

If you want to get to know a place better, go where

the locals go and dine where they eat their meals. This is a good pick as this place is obviously where the locals dine. The best choices are clams with pasta, squid ink pasta, seafood risotto and pickled anchovies. You may also try their tiramisu for dessert.

Calle della Madona, 594
Venezia, Italy
+39 041 522 3824

Bistrot De Venise

A restaurant that has both a a formal dining area and a casual, more relaxed environment. You can try their salami, proscuitto, cheeses, walnuts and honey accompanied by a bread basket (bread, focaccia and bread sticks). Simply great food with exceptional service.

San Marco, 4685
Calle dei Fabbri Venezia, Italy
+39 041 523 665

Al Colombo

This ristorante is situated very close to Rialto Bridge and has been famous since the end of 1700's. They have a wide selection of Italian wines and other international labels. The sumptuous dishes that they serve are truly delectable, like their whole sea bass with cherry tomatoes and seafood baked in foil.

San Marco 4619
Venezia, Italy
+39 041 522 2627

6 VENICE NIGHTLIFE

Venice Rialto Bridge at night. Photo by <u>*Lee Crowley*</u>

Molocinque

Formerly a theatre complex, this was transformed
in 1999 into a vast club in Venice mainland. It
features four themed party pavilions, each offering
a different type of music. Complete with a dozen
bars, a color-changing pool, and plenty of cushy
furniture to create a seductive lounge ambience,
this club is a posh destination for a fashionable and
flirtatious clientele in the mood to mingle and
dance. Hardcore party people should not miss this
place as it plays techno, pop, 70's, 80's and Latin
dance music. It's free before 10:30.

Via Elettricità, 8
Marghera VE, Italy
+39 041 538 4983

Orange
This venue has vibrant orange interiors, spicy
house music, and abstract art. One of the hippiest
bar in this side of town, it attracts an equally trendy
and energetic clientele. The music selection was
decent and there is both indoor and outdoor
seating. It's a good place to chill and enjoy a spritz.

Campo Santa Margherita, 3054a
Venezia, Italy
+39 041 523 4740

Bacaro Lounge

A cool, contemporary nightspot that is very
fashionable (it fits Milan or New York) in sleepy
Venice. A buzzing cocktail bar with a spectacular
glass staircase lined with hundreds of bottles of
wine, it has a cool and funky atmosphere playing
jazz music. One of the favorite bars in Venice,
Bacaro offers great food plus excellent service.

San Marco, 1345
Venezia, Italy
+39 041 296 0687

Margaret Duchamp

This is a cafe-brasserie located in the dynamic Campo Santa Margherita. It is open until 2am and really comes to life after midnight. Its an interesting cafe in a relatively quiet section of Venice touting minimalist decor that draws young and trendy crowds. Good for people watching while having a good chat with friends over drinks, it also offers light snacks. Prices are very reasonable.

Campo Santa Margherita, 3019
Venezia, Italy
+39 041 528 6255

7 BEST PLACES TO STAY (LUXURIOUS, MID-RANGE, BUDGET)

Venice. Photo by <u>Laiwan Ng</u>

Luxurious

The Gritti Palace

This is a luxurious accommodation with world-class facilities and amenities. You'll feel like nobility, and will be treated like royalty. This unique facility offers traditional Venetian style and elegance located on the enchanting Grand Canal. It was built in 1525 and was the private residence of the Doge of Venice, Andrea Gritti. It is still preserved and has been remodelled offering all the amenities and services for a comfortable stay. Carved flowers will greet you as you are ushered into your well appointed room over looking the Grand Canal. Simply put? Old world charm.

Campo Santa Maria del Giglio 2467, 30124 Venice
00 39 041 794611

The St. Regis Venice San Clemente Palace

A beautiful and charming hotel in a private island location, away from the hustle and bustle of Venice. Rooms are spacious and extremely luxurious and the hotel offers free breakfast and 24-hour room service. If you are in need of rest and relaxation you can find a sauna, an outdoor tennis court and a steam room on offer. Be sure to leave some room for your swimsuit as this hotel features a seasonal outdoor pool to unwind. Guests wishing to relax with a drink will surely want to visit the bar/lounge.

Isola di San Clemente 1, 30214 Venice
+39 041 475 0111

Mid-range

Al Ponte Antico

Another luxurious hotel located along the Grand Canal, it has breathtaking views over the Rialto Bridge. Occupying a little Gothic Palazzo, the hotel has a gilded panel entrance and top of the class facilities and amenities. If you're after a rather different take on Venetian baroque excesses and a truly warm welcome with endless helpful advice, then Al Ponte Antico will suit you just fine.

Camaregio 5768, Calle dell 'Aseo, Venice
+39 041 241 1944

Hotel Le Isole

A charming small hotel with classic Venetian style and contemporary design, it is located very close to Piazza San Marco. It welcomes guests inside the 16th century palazzo del sestiere of the Castel. This hotel's prime location brings you close to the city's main attractions. It has an intimate and familiar atmosphere with a cordial, multilingual staff. This hotel also offers world-class facilities and amenities.

Castello 4661, Fondamenta del vin, 30122 Venice
+39 041 522 8911

Budget

Hotel Caprera

A family-run hotel with personalized service. This hotel is closed to major tourist attractions like Palazzo Labia, St. Mary of the Friars, and Ca' d'Oro. Just nearby are Rialto Bridge and Squero di San Trovaso. Rooms are very comfortable and clean. The staff are very friendly and attentive. This hotel is in a quaint, small alley location and provides complimentary internet access, a 24-hour front desk, and other hotel amenities.

Cannaregio 219, 30121 Venice
+39 041 715271

Rio Venezia Hotel

Located in the heart of Venice, several rooms in this hotel were once occupied by the famous musical composer Antonio Vivaldi. Run by a friendly and knowledgeable team, it offers charming, recently refurbished environment. Rates are very affordable and you will get true value for your money.

Castello 4358, Campo SS. Filippo e Giacommo, 30122 Venice
+39 041 5226230

8 OTHER RECOMMENDED PLACES TO VISIT

Giudecca

This an island off the beaten track. A charming, truly Venetian area less frequented by tourists.The southern part of this island has a sequence of gardens with a breathtaking panorama of the lagoon. This is where the nobles of yesteryears enjoyed their time in summer and autumn. Nowadays, it is one of the most inhabited areas of Venice.

San Giorgio Maggiore

Take a quick vaporetto ride to see this magnificent structure. This is an isalnd church built by Palladio, decorated by Tintoretto and Bassano, and offering great views from the campanile.

One of the best architectural treasures of Venice, it has a gleaming white facade and a lithe brick and marble bell tower that seems as though it's floating in the middle of the Bacino San Marco, supported

on its own tiny island, just a few hundred yards off
St. Mark's Square.

Arsenale

This is a place in Castello where warships were
made. Considered to be a gem, it kept the
Venetian's hold in power and supremacy during the
medieval and Rennaisance period. It was within the
walls of this edifice that the galleys were built. The
arsenale is like a mini city, where one can enter via
grand crenellated towers of terracotta brick which
marks the opening of the canal. Visit the Naval
history museum to see warships, weapons, maps,
and gondolas from over the centuries. You can also
see the ceremonial barge used by the doges.

Interesting Facts About Venice

- Venice contains approximately 7,000
  chimneys. They come in 10 different
  styles and shapes.
- As for their bell towers, there are 170 of
  them. In Venetian culture, bell towers
  were a very important form of
  communication. San Marco is one of the
  tallest.
- San Marco is 275 feet tall. Sadly, the tower
  collapsed in 1902. No humans were hurt
  in the accident, but there was causality
  with the caretaker's cat. Nevertheless,
  the tower was rebuilt to look exactly like
  it did when it was first constructed.

- Venice has 177 canals and over 400 bridges.
- The Grand Canal is the region's largest. Possessing a unique S-shape, the canal splits the city in half.
- Three of the city's bridges have been around since ancient times: Rialto, Accademia and the Scalzi (which is also known as the Ferrovia).These bridges seem sturdier than some of the more modern bridges constructed in the city. Consider the Calatrava which is only four years in age. It is already starting to decay.
- Venice is divided by quarters. There are six altogether.
- The city has 350 gondolas.

Each year the town receives 18 million tourists. This equates to approximately 50,000 visitors each day.

CONCLUSION

A visit to Venice will give you an experience that won't be easily forgotten. Its irresistible landscapes, the grandiosity of its architecture, and its flamboyant structures, will make it easy for you to fall in love with this place. As the pages of history unfold before your very eyes, you will be entranced in its magic.

Venice truly offers one of Europe's best sightseeing experiences and each part of this floating city has its own story. Behind its splendid and impressive facade is a rich history of an intriguing and at times, complex past. As you explore its inner recesses, don't be afraid to get lost. The city is like a maze and finding your way around as you explore the little nook and cranny of the city will just add up to the excitement. Head to where there are no crowds and cruise its lagoons as well as the Grand Canal, which serves as the city's main boulevard winding through the city. Let your senses be awaken by the sight, sound, feel and taste of Venice. The rewards of endless discoveries will be completely worth it.

MORE FROM THIS AUTHOR

Below you'll find some of our other books that are popular on Amazon and Kindle as well. Alternatively, you can visit our author page on Amazon to see other work done by us.

3 Day Guide to Berlin: A 72-hour definitive guide on what to see, eat and enjoy in Berlin, Germany

3 Day Guide to Vienna: A 72-hour definitive guide on what to see, eat and enjoy in Vienna Austria

3 Day Guide to Santorini: A 72-hour definitive guide on what to see, eat and enjoy in Santorini Greece

3 Day Guide to Provence: A 72-hour definitive guide on what to see, eat and enjoy in Provence, France

3 Day Guide to Istanbul: A 72-hour definitive guide on what to see, eat and enjoy in Istanbul, Turkey

3 Day Guide to Budapest: A 72-hour Definitive Guide on What to See, Eat and Enjoy in Budapest, Hungary

3 Day Guide to Venice: A 72-hour Definitive Guide on What to See, Eat and Enjoy in Venice, Italy

Printed in Great Britain
by Amazon